"Lift every voice and sing
Till earth and heaven ring,
Ring with the harmonies of Liberty;
Let our rejoicing rise
High as the listening skies,
Let it resound loud as the rolling sea."

—JAMES WELDON JOHNSON,
FROM "LIFT EVERY VOICE AND SING"

THE HARLEM RENAISSANCE: A CELEBRATION OF CREATIVITY

BY LUCIA RAATMA

The Child's World

Published in the United States of America by The Child's World®
PO Box 326
Chanhassen, MN 55317-0326
800-599-READ
www.childsworld.com

The Child's World®: Mary Berendes, Publishing Director
Editorial Directions, Inc.: E. Russell Primm, Emily Dolbear, Lucia Raatma
and Sarah E. De Capua, Editors; Linda S. Koutris, Photo Selector; Alice Flanagan,
Photo Research; Red Line Editorial, Fact Research; Tim Griffin/IndexServ, Indexer;
Melissa McDaniel, Proofreader

Cover photograph: The Cotton Club in Harlem, 1932/ © Frank Driggs Collection/Hulton
Archive/Getty Images

Interior photographs ©: RCA Victor/AP/Wide World Photos: 26; Schomburg Center, The New York
Public Library/Art Resource, NY: 30; Beinecke Rare Book & Manuscript Library, Yale University Library: 14,
22, 32, 33, 35; Corbis: 9, 10, 13, 29 top left, 31; Underwood and Underwood/Corbis: 6; Bettmann/Corbis: 12,
19; Bradley Smith/Corbis: 29 bottom right; Hulton Archive/Getty Images: 11, 16, 23, 27; Frank Driggs
Collection/Hulton Archive/Getty Images: 2, 25, 28; Stock Montage/Hulton Archive/Getty Images: 8; George
Eastman House/Nickolas Muray/Hulton Archive/Getty Images: 15; Library of Congress: 21; The Gibson
Studio/ Schomburg Center for Research in Black Culture, Prints & Photographs Division, The New York
Public Library: 17; Schomburg Center for Research in Black Culture, Prints & Photographs Division,
The New York Public Library: 18, 20.

Library of Congress Cataloging-in-Publication Data
Raatma, Lucia.
The Harlem Renaissance : a celebration of creativity / by Lucia Raatma.
p. cm.
Includes index.
Summary: An introduction to the period in the 1920s known as the Harlem Renaissance,
when the expression of African American creativity in many forms flourished.
ISBN 1-56766-645-0 (Library Bound : alk. paper)
1. African Americans—Intellectual life—20th century—Juvenile literature.
2. Harlem Renaissance—Juvenile literature. 3. African Americans—History—1877–1964—
Juvenile literature. 4. African American arts—History—20th century—Juvenile literature.
5. Harlem (New York, N.Y.)—Intellectual life—20th century—Juvenile literature.
6. African American intellectuals—New York (State)—New York—Biography—Juvenile literature.
[1. Harlem Renaissance. 2. African American arts. 3. African Americans—History—1877–1964.] I. Title.
E185.6 .R15 2002
700'.92'39607307471—dc21

2001008120

Contents

PAUL ROBESON IS BEST REMEMBERED FOR HIS STARRING ROLE IN *SHOW BOAT*. DURING THE HARLEM RENAISSANCE, HE IMPRESSED AUDIENCES WITH HIS REMARKABLE SIGNING VOICE AND ACTING ABILITY.

A Special Time

The 1920s were important years in the history of the United States. It was a **decade** of wealth and happiness for many people. Women cut their hair in styles called bobs, and they wore shorter dresses. People enjoyed entertainment of all kinds. They listened to **jazz**, and they danced the Charleston.

During this same period, some African-Americans also experienced a special time. It was a time of remarkable creativity for African-Americans working in the arts. Black writers such as Langston Hughes, Countee Cullen, and Zora Neale Hurston wrote moving poems, plays, and books about African-American life. Jazz musicians such as Louis Armstrong and Duke Ellington had legions of fans all around the world. And actors such as Paul Robeson starred on Broadway and won the hearts of audiences.

Much of this activity took place in New York City, specifically in Harlem. So these years came to be known as the Harlem **Renaissance**. But the influence of the Harlem Renaissance touched the lives of people from all backgrounds—in New York and throughout the United States.

Making a Home in Harlem

The United States entered World War I (1914–1918) in 1917. Many Americans feared **communism**, which had been established in the Soviet Union. So President Woodrow Wilson told the American people that fighting the war was necessary to protect American **democracy**. The democracy in the United States, was far from perfect, however.

African-Americans had gained their freedom from slavery after the Civil War (1861–1865), but they were still not treated the way white Americans were. **Segregation** laws existed in many states. Blacks and whites had separate waiting rooms in bus and train stations. They had separate entrances to movie theaters and public buildings. They even had separate water fountains. Finding good-paying jobs was harder for black Americans than it was for white Americans. And some groups, such as the **Ku Klux Klan**, actually believed that whites were better than blacks. Race **riots** occurred all over the country, with blacks and whites fighting one another.

WOODROW WILSON WAS PRESIDENT DURING WORLD WAR I. HE SAID THAT THE UNITED STATES HAD TO ENTER THE WAR TO PROTECT DEMOCRACY.

FOR MANY YEARS, BLACKS IN MANY STATES WERE FORCED TO USE SEPARATE ENTRANCES, WAITING ROOMS, AND EVEN DRINKING FOUNTAINS. SUCH PRACTICES WERE OUTLAWED BY THE CIVIL RIGHTS ACT OF 1964.

EVEN AFTER FIGHTING FOR THE UNITED STATES IN
WORLD WAR I, BLACK SOLDIERS WERE GREETED
WITH DISCRIMINATION AT HOME.

In spite of this unfairness, African-Americans did their part in World War I. Black men fought in Europe and risked their lives for the American cause. But when they returned to the United States after the war, nothing had changed. They were not respected, just as before the war. Race riots continued, and much blood was shed. The Red Summer of 1919 was a violent and horrible time.

The well-known scholar and writer W. E. B. Du Bois wrote about the problems faced by African-Americans in an important magazine called *Crisis*. He urged black Americans to take pride in themselves. And he argued that black Americans should have the same rights as whites and people of other backgrounds did. He disagreed with some black leaders of the time. For instance, Booker T. Washington, who founded the Tuskegee Institute, believed in **compromise**. He felt that blacks and whites could get along. But he believed that blacks should try to live like whites and be accommodating to white society. Du Bois believed in holding on to African-American traditions and ideas.

His work eventually led to the **civil rights** movement of the 1950s and 1960s.

BOOKER T. WASHINGTON WAS THE FOUNDER OF THE TUSKEGEE INSTITUTE. HE WORKED HARD TO EDUCATE AFRICAN-AMERICANS, BUT MANY FELT HE TOO EASILY COMPROMISED WITH WHITE LEADERS.

From 1900 to 1930, a large number of African-Americans left the South and moved north. They felt that there were more jobs in the North. And they hoped that they would be treated better than they were in the South. Many of these people made their new homes in Harlem. This section of Manhattan centered on Seventh Avenue and 125th Street and spread about 2 miles (3.2 kilometers) from that center.

The streets of Harlem could be crowded and noisy. But those streets were also full of life and opportunity. Many African-Americans felt instantly at home when they arrived in Harlem. For many, it was clearly the best place to be.

New Voices in Literature

One of the first black writers to have an audience of both black and white readers was Claude McKay. He was born in Jamaica and moved to Harlem in 1917. After the Red Summer of 1919, he wrote a powerful group of poems. His book, called *Harlem Shadows,* was published in 1922. Before that, McKay's work had appeared in the *Crisis* and he had made a reputation in the literary world. He was probably the first well-known writer of the Harlem Renaissance.

CLAUDE MCKAY WAS BORN IN JAMAICA BUT MOVED TO HARLEM IN HIS TWENTIES. HE WAS A WELL-KNOWN WRITER DURING THE HARLEM RENAISSANCE AND A STRONG VOICE FOR BLACK AMERICANS.

LIKE MANY OTHER BLACK ARTISTS OF THE 1920s, CLAUDE McKAY FELT A POWERFUL BOND WITH HARLEM. HIS BOOK *HOME TO HARLEM* WAS THE FIRST BOOK BY A HARLEM WRITER TO MAKE THE BEST-SELLER LIST.

McKay was interested in the ideals of communism. Though many viewed communism as totally negative, it attracted people of various backgrounds, including a number of African-Americans. They had their reasons. In communism, for example, there was no **racism**. There was no unemployment either. And in theory, there was no hunger or **poverty**. McKay wanted to see communism for himself so, during the 1920s, he traveled to the Soviet Union. Then he moved to France and continued to write about American life and Harlem. His autobiography, *A Long Way from Home*, was published in 1937.

Probably the best-known writer of the Harlem Renaissance was Langston Hughes. A gifted poet, Hughes also wrote plays, novels, and opera **librettos**. His first important poem was "The Negro Speaks of Rivers," which was published in the *Crisis*. After attending Columbia University briefly in 1921 and 1922, he worked on ships that sailed to Africa and Europe. He saw how the rest of the world treated blacks, and he wanted the United States to change. He continued to write while he traveled.

LANGSTON HUGHES WAS AN IMPORTANT WRITER OF THE HARLEM RENAISSANCE. HE LIVED IN NEW YORK CITY AND WASHINGTON, D.C., BUT ALSO SPENT TIME TRAVELING THE WORLD.

By the time Hughes arrived in Harlem in 1924, he was a celebrity. Though he was popular, he often felt alone and separate from others. He used the rhythms and sounds of **blues** and jazz music to make his poetry come alive. "The Weary Blues" is a poem he wrote about his own feelings of loneliness. It won a contest run by *Opportunity* magazine in 1925.

Hughes was one of the first African-Americans to earn a living as a writer. He traveled often. And he won cash prizes from contests and grants. He also became good friends with Carl Van Vechten. Van Vechten was a writer and critic who admired Hughes's work. He helped the young writer get his books published. He also offered Hughes advice and support. After the Harlem Renaissance, Hughes continued to write until his death in 1967. His time in Harlem proved to be very influential. It was the starting point of a brilliant career.

CARL VAN VECHTEN, A NOTED WRITER AND CRITIC, OFFERED HELP AND ENCOURAGEMENT TO THE ARTISTS OF THE HARLEM RENAISSANCE.

Countee Cullen was a good friend to Hughes. This poet was first published at age fifteen. He was inspired by the English poet John Keats. Though Cullen wrote about the black experience in America, his work influenced people of all races. He believed that art should speak to everyone. His poetry collections *Copper Sun* and *The Ballad of the Brown Girl* were published in 1927. And his last collection, *The Black Christ and Other Poems*, was released in 1929. He went on to write in other forms, including children's books and novels.

COUNTEE CULLEN WAS AN IMPORTANT WRITER WHO WAS INFLUENCED BY ENGLISH POET JOHN KEATS. HIS WORK TOUCHED READERS OF ALL RACES.

Zora Neale Hurston was a flashy and talented writer who got her start during the Harlem Renaissance. She studied anthropology in college, and she was very interested in cultures throughout the world. Hurston dressed in colorful and elaborate outfits and sometimes wore a turban. Her outspoken nature was often criticized by other writers but she was very popular among people who threw parties in Harlem. And as a writer she had great success. Her short story "Drenched in Light" appeared in *Opportunity* magazine in 1924. She also won a prize from that publication for her play *Color Struck*. On a few occasions, she wrote plays with Langston Hughes. After the Harlem Renaissance, Hurston wrote *Mules and Men*, a book about African-American folklore. And she continued to create important works about African-American life.

ZORA NEALE HURSTON WAS A FLASHY AND OUTSPOKEN WRITER. SHE WROTE SHORT STORIES, PLAYS, AND OTHER WORKS ABOUT AFRICAN-AMERICAN LIFE.

Writer Jean Toomer was a gifted novelist. In 1923, his book *Cane* was hailed as a masterpiece. It was inspired by a visit Toomer made to the rural South. He was touched by the beautiful countryside. He loved the sounds of **gospel** music sung by African-American women there. Though he appreciated this **heritage**, he had trouble with his own background. His mother was white, and his father was of mixed race. This combination made Toomer quite light-skinned, and he could "pass" as white. Sometimes he felt lost between the black world and the white world. Toomer traveled in France for a time, and when he returned to New York he decided to leave Harlem. Instead, he spent most of his time in Greenwich Village. There he socialized with white artists and writers. The people of Harlem felt they had lost an important voice.

COMING FROM A MIXED-RACE BACKGROUND, JEAN TOOMER SOMETIMES FELT LOST BETWEEN THE BLACK WORLD AND THE WHITE WORLD. HIS 1923 NOVEL, *CANE*, WAS CLAIMED A MASTERPIECE.

Many of these and other Harlem Renaissance writers owed their success to W. E. B. Du Bois. As editor of the *Crisis*, the magazine of the National Association for the Advancement of Colored People (NAACP), he often played a part in publishing the early work of these writers.

Jessie Fauset, an editor at the publication, also had a key role in these writers' success. She was frequently the first to recognize the talent of poets and short-story writers. Many of them found her to be more approachable than Du Bois, so she proved to be an encouraging force in their work. She was known to hold gatherings for writers at her 142nd Street apartment, serving as adviser and mentor to them.

In addition to being a fine editor, Fauset was a writer as well. She published her first novel, *There Is Confusion*, in 1924. Other novels included *Plum Bun* and *The Chinaberry Tree*. Though her books received mixed reviews, some of her characters were most memorable.

JESSIE FAUSET, LITERARY EDITOR FOR THE *CRISIS*, ENCOURAGED THE WORK OF MANY IMPORTANT BLACK WRITERS. IT WAS SHE WHO OFTEN DISCOVERED NEW TALENT AND OFFERED ADVICE.

James Weldon Johnson was also important to the literary brilliance of the Harlem Renaissance. He was a writer and editor who was a leader in the NAACP. He often edited collections of African-American poetry and helped to get the works published. Among these works was *The Book of American Negro Poetry*, which he edited in 1922. Later, with his brother Rosamond, Johnson compiled a collection of Negro spirituals and wrote music for them. He also wrote the words to the hymn "Lift Every Voice and Sing," which he and Rosamond put to music.

Johnson portrayed the problems experienced by people of mixed race in *The Autobiography of an Ex-Colored Man*. He published this book anonymously in 1912 and then under his own name in 1927. Also that year, he published *God's Trombones: Seven Negro Sermons in Verse*. Johnson spent his life creating literary works and improving the work of others. He felt that African-Americans could advance in society by being successful in art and literature.

A LEADER IN THE NAACP, JAMES WELDON JOHNSON WORKED TO IMPROVE THE LIVES OF AFRICAN-AMERICANS. HIMSELF A WRITER AND EDITOR, JOHNSON BELIEVED SUCCESS IN ART AND LITERATURE WOULD HELP BLACK AMERICANS PROGRESS IN SOCIETY.

Scholar and professor Alain Locke was an adviser to many of the Harlem writers. He graduated from Harvard and came from a well-educated family. Locke was the first person to use the term "the New Negro" to describe the young artists of the Harlem Renaissance. He encouraged African-Americans to celebrate their background to bring about change in the United States.

Another important writer of the era was Arna Bontemps. He paid tribute to the African-American culture through his essays, novels, and children's books. Recording history and writing books for children were important goals for Bontemps. After the Harlem Renaissance, he wrote about the people who had played a role in that period. He also worked with friends Langston Hughes and Countee Cullen on a number of projects, including collections and plays.

ALAIN LOCKE, A SCHOLAR AND PROFESSOR, SERVED AS ADVISER TO MANY HARLEM WRITERS. HE ENCOURAGED AFRICAN-AMERICANS TO CELEBRATE THEIR BACKGROUNDS THROUGH THEIR ART.

On Stages, in Clubs, and at Galleries

The artistic talent of the Harlem Renaissance was not limited to writers. New voices in drama, music, and the visual arts also had great influence during that period.

Paul Robeson is probably the most famous black actor of that era. He earned degrees from both Rutgers University and Columbia Law School. And he was the first black university football player to be named all-American. In 1924, Robeson starred in two Eugene O'Neill plays, *All God's Chillun Got Wings* and *The Emperor Jones*. He had a beautiful singing voice for which he became well known. He was a popular concert singer of the era, and he also starred in the film *Body and Soul*.

PAUL ROBESON, AN ACCOMPLISHED STUDENT AND FINE ATHLETE, EARNED FAME ON THE AMERICAN STAGE. BUT AFTER EXPRESSING INTEREST IN COMMUNIST IDEAS, HE FELL OUT OF FAVOR IN THE UNITED STATES.

After the Harlem Renaissance, Paul Robeson continued to act and sing. One of his best-remembered roles was in *Show Boat* in 1936. In that production, he sang "Old Man River," a song often associated with him. Later in his life, he was a friend to the communist Soviet Union. For this, he lost much of his acceptance by Americans.

The 1920s were marked not just by the Harlem Renaissance. These years were also known as the Jazz Age. Jazz began in the late 1890s and early 1900s, mostly in New Orleans. This type of music is best recognized by its racial **diversity** and its complicated rhythms. Writer Langston Hughes embraced jazz music, and some of his poetry even expressed the patterns and sound of jazz. The spirit of jazz music seemed to celebrate the freedom and the experimentation of the Harlem Renaissance. As an art form, jazz reached its peak in Harlem during the Roaring Twenties. But today it continues to thrive and evolve, and many consider jazz to be the most genuine reflection ever created of African-American life.

Music halls in Harlem usually included a restaurant and bar, in addition to nightly music shows. Probably the most famous was the Cotton Club. Bandleader Duke Ellington was the main attraction there. Ellington's band consisted of trumpet players and pianists, drummers and **percussionists**. His radio broadcasts from the Cotton Club earned him national attention. During his lifetime, he composed at least 2,000 works. After the Harlem Renaissance, he toured the United States with his band. Ellington was best known for "It Don't Mean a Thing (If It Ain't Got That Swing)," "Take the 'A' Train," and "Don't Get Around Much Anymore." In 1969, he received the Presidential Medal of Freedom. And during the course of his career, he won eleven Grammy Awards.

DUKE ELLINGTON AND HIS BAND. THEIR RADIO BROADCASTS FROM HARLEM'S COTTON CLUB BROUGHT THEM NATIONAL ATTENTION.

LOUIS ARMSTRONG GOT HIS START IN NEW ORLEANS, HIS HOMETOWN, BUT MOVED TO NEW YORK CITY IN 1924. FAMOUS FOR HIS TRUMPET PLAYING, HE EARNED AN INTERNATIONAL FOLLOWING.

Another respected musician of the time was Louis Armstrong. This trumpet player got his start in New Orleans and moved to New York City in 1924. There he joined the band of Fletcher Henderson, a piano player. He then formed his own band and worked with singers such as Bessie Smith. In the 1930s and 1940s, Armstrong toured Europe and gained an international audience. He appeared in a number of films and received a Grammy Lifetime Achievement Award in 1972, the year after his death.

Fletcher Henderson performed with his Rainbow Orchestra at a club called the Savoy. The radio broadcasts from the Savoy were very popular with the American public.

THE SAVOY, ONE OF HARLEM'S MOST FAMOUS CLUBS. FLETCHER HENDERSON'S RAINBOW ORCHESTRA OFTEN PERFORMED THERE.

essie Smith was born in the South but moved to New York City in 1923. There she recorded with Armstrong as well as with Benny Goodman and James P. Johnson. Known as "Empress of the Blues," Smith had a deep and powerful voice. She was said to be earning $2,000 a week in the 1920s, a huge amount of money at that time. Later, she turned away from music. She died in Mississippi in 1937 after a car accident.

Musician and composer W. C. Handy moved to New York City in 1920. He founded a publishing and sheet music company. Some of his best-known songs are "St. Louis Blues" and "Beale Street Blues," which both became classics. He wrote his lyrics in Negro dialect, believing that was the truest way to portray the African-American experience.

VOCALIST BESSIE SMITH PERFORMED WITH LOUIS ARMSTRONG AND MANY OTHER MUSICIANS. HER POWERFUL SINGING EARNED HER $2,000 A WEEK.

A famous pianist of the Harlem Renaissance was Jelly Roll Morton. An important jazz musician, he gained most of his fame in New Orleans. During the 1920s, he toured all over the country and often performed in Harlem.

Billie Holiday, one of the greatest jazz singers of all time, moved to New York City in the late 1920s. She got her start started singing in Harlem nightclubs, though she wasn't well known until the 1930s. Later in her career, she performed with the bands of Artie Shaw and Count Basie as well as with saxophonist Lester Young.

JELLY ROLL MORTON (ABOVE) EARNED FAME IN NEW ORLEANS BUT ALSO PERFORMED IN HARLEM. BILLIE HOLIDAY (RIGHT) LAUNCHED HER REMARKABLE CAREER BY SINGING IN HARLEM NIGHTCLUBS.

During the Harlem Renaissance, nightclubs were definitely swinging and humming to the sounds of black America. Both black and white audiences found the sound of jazz to be infectious and intriguing. The 1920s was an exciting, creative time for black musicians, a decade that changed American music forever.

The Harlem Renaissance also saw the rise of many notable painters and sculptors. Aaron Douglas used the style of **primitive** African statues in his paintings. His murals and portraits illustrate the social and cultural progress of black America. His work inspired many other African-American artists to express themselves on canvas.

The Negro in Africa, a famous work by artist Aaron Douglas. Douglas used a primitive style to express himself on canvas.

Augusta Savage was a sculptor who lived and worked in Harlem. Among other works, she created a **bust** of W. E. B. Du Bois, which was presented to the New York Public Library in 1923. She also did a bust of Marcus Garvey, an important black **activist** of the early twentieth century and founder of the United Negro Improvement Association. In 1932, she founded the Savage Studio of Arts and Crafts in Harlem. Five years later, she became the director of the Harlem Community Art Center.

In spite of these successes, she had a hard life. She was both widowed and divorced by age thirty-one. She supported her daughter as well as her parents and numerous brothers and sisters. At one point, Augusta Savage she was denied entrance to a famous French art school, perhaps only because of her race. But, like many other artists of the Harlem Renaissance, Savage used her art to tell us about her life. In her statues, she told the stories of herself. Her art is a treasured expression of black America.

SCULPTOR AUGUSTA SAVAGE WAS AN IMPORTANT FORCE IN THE ART WORLD. HER BUSTS OF W. E. B. DU BOIS AND MARCUS GARVEY ARE WELL KNOWN.

The End of an Era

The Harlem Renaissance was driven by the talents of many young writers, musicians, and visual artists. But this movement was also made possible by a number of **patrons** who helped support the creative minds financially. Most notable was Carl Van Vechten, who advised Langston Hughes as well as novelists Rudolph Fisher and Nella Larsen.

An influential black woman of the decade was A'Lelia Walker. Her mother was one of the country's first millionaires. After her mother's death, Walker received a great deal of money. She used some of it to throw glamorous parties for both black and white **intellectuals**. A fashionable woman, she enjoyed entertaining and loved supporting the arts. Writers and musicians often gathered at her home. And in 1927, she opened a club called the Dark Tower on West 136th Street.

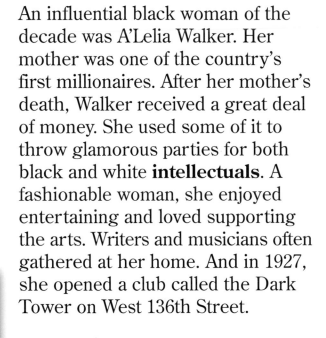

NOVELIST NELLA LARSEN WAS ONE WRITER WHO WAS ADVISED BY CARL VAN VECHTEN. SHE OFTEN WROTE UNDER DIFFERENT NAMES AND LED A MYSTERIOUS LIFE.

Another well-known patron of the era was Charlotte Osgood Mason. She gave money and support to Langston Hughes, Zora Neale Hurston, and Aaron Douglas. Unfortunately, she thought that she was superior to these artists. Often, she was critical of their work and tried to control what they produced. This attitude eventually led to splits with all three artists.

An important organization for Harlem Renaissance artists was the Harmon Foundation. Created by William E. Harmon and later run by Mary Beattie Brady, the foundation offered awards for black artists and provided publicity for them.

A'LELIA WALKER WAS A STYLISH WOMAN WHO ENJOYED THROWING GLAMOROUS PARTIES DURING THE HARLEM RENAISSANCE. SHE ALSO OWNED A CLUB CALLED THE DARK TOWER.

The creative work produced during the Harlem Renaissance was powerful and important. Yet it was a complicated time for many African-Americans. They found themselves writing, singing, and painting in hopes of pleasing white critics. They worried about what white audiences would think of them. They were anxious about keeping their white patrons happy.

Many leaders in both black and white society voiced concern about this problem. They urged black artists to be true to themselves. They said that black creativity should not be controlled by white opinion. Many African-Americans tried to remain loyal to themselves, but the influence of white society was very strong.

Even these wealthy patrons and strong-minded critics could not prevent the changes brought about by the **Great Depression**. On October 29, 1929, the stock market crashed. Suddenly, the Roaring Twenties screeched to a halt. The **prosperity** of the decade disappeared overnight. And soon the nation was marked by unemployment, homelessness, and poverty.

Despite these problems, many of the talented people of the Harlem Renaissance continued to write, make music, and create art long after the 1920s. And their work influenced other black artists for generations to come. But by 1930, the wonderful, energy-filled Harlem Renaissance had come to an end.

OPPOSITE: *THE PRODIGAL SON*, A WORK BY AARON DOUGLAS THAT SYMBOLIZED THE ART, MUSIC, AND PROSPERITY OF THE HARLEM RENAISSANCE.

Timeline

1910	W. E. B. Du Bois becomes the director of research of the NAACP and editor of its magazine, the *Crisis*.
1912	Claude McKay publishes two collections of poetry, *Songs of Jamaica* and *Constab Ballads*.
1914–1918	World War I rages in Europe.
1917	The United States enters World War I.
1919	Race riots take place in America during the Red Summer; Jessie Fauset moves Harlem and takes the job of literary editor for the *Crisis*.
1920	Marcus Garvey organizes the first convention of the United Negro Improvement Association.
1920–1925	More than 2 million African-Americans move from the South to the North
1921	The musical *Shuffle Along* opens and marks the beginning of the Jazz Age.
1922	Claude McKay's *Harlem Shadows* is published; James Weldon Johnson edits *The Book of American Negro Poetry*.
1923	Singer Bessie Smith moves to New York City; Augusta Savage's bust of W. E. B. Du Bois is presented to the New York Public Library; Duke Ellington moves to New York City and begins playing with the Washingtonians at the Hollywood Club.
1924	Langston Hughes returns to the United States after traveling abroad; Paul Robeson stars in *All God's Chillun Got Wings* and *The Emperor Jones*; Louis Armstrong moves to New York City; Duke Ellington plays at the Cotton Club, and later the Duke Ellington Orchestra becomes the house band for the club.
1925	Langston Hughes wins an *Opportunity* magazine prize for "The Weary Blues."
1926	W. C. Handy publishes *Blues Anthology* and tours with Jelly Roll Morton; Zora Neale Hurston, Langston Hughes, Aaron Douglas, and others found a magazine called *Fire!!* but it fails after only one issue.
1927	Countee Cullen's *Copper Sun* and *The Ballad of the Brown Girl* are published; Arna Bontemps wins a poetry contest sponsored by the *Crisis*.
1929	Countee Cullen's *The Black Christ and Other Poems* is published; the stock market crashes on October 29 and the Great Depression begins.
1939	James Weldon Johnson, who died in a 1938 car accident, is honored at the World's Fair with a sculpture by Augusta Savage titled *Lift Every Voice and Sing*.

Glossary

activist (AK-ti-vist)
An activist is someone who works to support a specific issue. Some civil rights activists got their start during the Harlem Renaissance.

blues (BLOOZ)
Blues is a type of music that is often marked by sad, slow lyrics. Both jazz and blues were popular during the 1920s.

bust (BUHST)
A bust is a sculpture of the upper part of a person's body. Augusta Savage created busts of Marcus Garvey and W. E. B. Du Bois.

civil rights (SIV-il RYTS)
Civil rights are the rights of all citizens. Many famous African-Americans fought for civil rights during the twentieth century.

communism (KOM-yuh-niz-uhm)
Communism is an economic system in which the government owns everything. Some people find communism appealing because in that system there is no unemployment or racism.

compromise (KOM-pruh-myz)
In a compromise, both sides agree to accept something other than what they originally wanted.

decade (DEK-ayd)
A decade is a period of ten years. The Harlem Renaissance took place during the decade of the 1920s.

democracy (di-MOK-ruh-see)
In a democracy, people elect their leaders by voting.

diversity (di-VUR-suh-tee)
A diversity is a variety. The Harlem Renaissance celebrated diversity in its literature, art, and music.

gospel (GOSS-puhl)
Gospel music has religious lyrics. Many writers have been inspired by the words of gospel songs.

Great Depression (GRAYT di-PRESH-uhn)
The Great Depression was a period in U.S. history marked by unemployment, poverty, and homelessness. It marked the end of the Harlem Renaissance.

heritage (HER-uh-tij)
A group's heritage includes traditions that are passed down from generation to generation. African-Americans are often proud of their heritage.

intellectuals (in-tuh-LEK-choo-uhls)
Intellectuals spend a lot of time thinking and studying. Many intellectuals enjoyed the creativity of the Harlem Renaissance.

jazz (JAZ)
Jazz is a type of music known for its rhythms and improvisation. The Jazz Age got its true beginning during the 1920s.

Glossary

Ku Klux Klan (KOO KLUKS KLAN)
The Ku Klux Klan is a group that hates people in minority groups. The freedom and creativity of the Harlem Renaissance was seen as threatening by the Ku Klux Klan.

librettos (leh-BREH-tohs)
Librettos are books that contain the texts of musical works, such as operas.

patrons (PAY-truhns)
Patrons are people who help a cause, usually by giving money. Some patrons of Harlem artists encouraged their work while others were too controlling.

percussionists (pur-KUH-shuh-nists)
Percussionists play musical instruments that are shaken, scraped, or tapped.Many Harlem musicians were fine percussionists.

poverty (POV-ur-tee)
Someone who lives in poverty has little money and very few possessions. For years after being freed from slavery, black Americans had to fight their way out of poverty.

primitive (PRIM-uh-tiv)
Something that is primitive is uncivilized or crude. A primitive culture is in an early stage of its development.

prosperity (pross-PERH-uh-tee)
Prosperity is the condition of being wealthy and successful. The Roaring Twenties marked a time of prosperity in the United States.

racism (RAYS-ihz-uhm)
Racism is the belief that one race is better than others. The history of the United States is scarred by racism.

renaissance (REN-uh-sahnss)
A renaissance is a time of dramatic, artistic, and creative development. The Harlem Renaissance of the 1920s was such a time.

riots (RYE-uhts)
Riots are events of violent, public discord. The United States has often experienced race riots in its history.

segregation (seg-ruh-GAY-shuhn)
Segregation is separating groups of people from one another. For many years, racial segregation was legal in the United States.

Index

FOR FURTHER READING

Books

Chambers, Veronica. *The Harlem Renaissance.* Broomall, Pa.: Chelsea House, 1998.

Haskins, Jim. *Black Stars of the Harlem Renaissance.* New York: John Wiley & Sons, 2002.

Sullivan, Charles, editor. *Children of Promise: African-American Literature and Art for Young People.* New York: Harry N. Abrams, 1991.

Web Sites

Visit our homepage for lots of links about the Harlem Renaissance: *http://www.childsworld.com/links.html*

Note to Parents, Teachers, and Librarians:
We routinely verify our Web links to make sure they're safe, active sites—so encourage your readers to check them out!

ABOUT THE AUTHOR

Lucia Raatma received her bachelor's degree in English literature from the University of South Carolina and her master's degree in cinema studies from New York University. After spending many years in Manhattan book publishing, she turned her interests to freelance writing, and she has since written a wide range of books for young people. When she is not researching or writing, she enjoys going to movies, playing tennis, practicing yoga, and spending time with her husband, daughter, and golden retriever. She lives in New York.